Independent Fluency Practice Passages

Fiction & Nonfiction

FLUENCY

Grade 1

Newmark™
LEARNING

Newmark Learning • 629 Fifth Avenue • Pelham, NY • 10803

Fluency Passage Reading Levels

The reading levels of the passages in each Independent Fluency Practice Series book span at least two and as many as five grades.

The purpose of including a wide range of reading levels is to accommodate students in Grades 1, 2, or 3 who read at different levels, and allow them to develop at their own pace. In addition, the wide range allows for students' natural growth and reading improvement during the school year. As students become better readers, they can practice with fluency passages at increasingly higher reading levels.

Book	Reading Levels	Grade-Level Equivalent
Grade 1 **Monologues & Dialogues**	D–E	K, 1—1st half
	F–G	1—1st half
	H–I	1—2nd half
Grade 1 **Fiction & Nonfiction**	J–K	2—1st half
	L–M	2—2nd half
Grade 2 **Monologues & Dialogues**	F–G	1—1st half
	H–I	1—2nd half
	J–K	2—1st half
Grade 2 **Fiction & Nonfiction**	L–M	2—2nd half
	N-O-P	3
Grade 3 **Monologues & Dialogues**	H–I	1—2nd half
	J–K	2—1st half
	L–M	2—2nd half
Grade 3 **Fiction & Nonfiction**	N-O-P	3
	Q–R	4

Table of Contents

Welcome to Newmark Learning's Independent Fluency Practice Passages Series. Each grade-level Fiction and Nonfiction title in this series provides 28 carefully leveled practice passages at a range of levels to accommodate on-, below-, and above-level readers. Each book comes with an audio CD that provides fluent readings of each passage so that students can listen and read along to build fluency and comprehension. All reading passages connect to grade-appropriate Science and Social Studies content or fiction genres.

Fluency Research

Fluency is the ability to read a text accurately and quickly. Fluent readers recognize words automatically. They group words into phrases to help them gain the meaning of what they read. Fluent readers also read aloud using prosody—the technical term for reading with expressiveness—with little or no effort.

Fluency is a vital skill because it directly relates to comprehension. Research from the National Reading Panel concludes that repeated oral reading practice at students' independent reading levels is essential to build fluency.

Getting Started:

❑ **Make copies of passages at the student's independent reading level.** You will find the reading level in the upper right corner of each passage.

❑ **Make a copy of the Fluency Self-Assessment Master Checklist and My Fluency Practice Graphs** (pages 61–63) for each passage. If possible, provide a folder in which to store the forms.

❑ **Make a copy of the "Student Instructions" on page 64.** Glue them onto a piece of cardboard.

❑ **Choose a place for the student to work.** Place the copied reading passages, self-assessment charts, graphs, student instructions, a portable CD player, and a stopwatch nearby.

❑ **Demonstrate each step.** Allow students to practice with your help until the process is automatic.

Water

Water is all around.

You can find water at the beach.

We use water to play.

You can find water at
a water fountain.

over →

 We use water to drink.

 You can find water in the bathroom.

 We use water to wash our hands.

 You can find water in the kitchen.

 We use water to cook.

 You can find water outside.

 We use water in the garden.

Water Fun

"Water, water, I love water!" said Lil. "I love to play in water."

"I love to play in the sprinkler," said Tina.

"I love to play in the pool," said Kim.

over →

"I love to play in the lake," said Shane.

"Water, water, I love water!" said Lil. "I love to play on water."

"How can you play *on* water?" asked Shane.

"Water can freeze," said Lil. "Then the water is ice. I can skate on ice!"

Here and There

I like to go to school.

I can walk to school.

I can ride my bike to school.

I like to go to my friend's house.

My mom takes me in a car.

A car can take you far away.

over

Sometimes I ride a bus to my friend's house. A bus can take you far away.

I like to go to my grandma's house. We take a train to her house. A train can take you far, far away.

Sometimes we take a plane to my grandma's house. A plane can take you far, far away.

My Toy Models

"Do you want to see
my models?" asked Shay.

"What is a model?" asked Jed.

"A model is small. But a
model looks like something
big," said Shay.

over

"I see a model truck," said Jed. "The model truck looks like your mom's big truck."

"Here is a model boat," said Shay.

"I like to ride on boats," said Jed. "I see a model horse. I like to ride on horses, too."

"Mom can take us to the farm. We can go in her big truck. We can ride big horses," said Shay.

At the Park

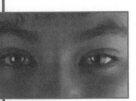

You are at the park.
What can you see?

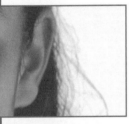

What can you hear?

What can you touch?

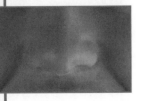

What can you smell?

over

What can you taste?

You see grass. You see trees.

You hear kids. You hear dogs.

You slide on the slide.
You swing on the swings.

You smell hot dogs.

Get a hot dog. Taste
the hot dog. Mmm!

Pizza Treat

"The pizza is here!" said Mom.

"The pizza looks good,"
said Bob.

"The pizza smells good,"
said Jamal.

over →

"Let's eat!" said Jane.

"The pizza will taste good," said Bob, Jamal, and Jane.

Mom cut the pizza. Mom cut eight slices. Bob, Jamal, and Jane took slices.

"Ouch!" said Bob, Jamal, and Jane.

Mom said, "The pizza is hot. Do not touch the pizza. Wait a little while. The pizza will still taste good."

Happy Birthday, Kim

Today is Kim's birthday.

Kim is having a party.

Kim's family is at
the birthday party.

over

Kim's friends are at the birthday party. Kim's friends will play games. Kim's friends will get prizes.

Kim's birthday cake has six candles. Kim will make a wish. Then Kim will blow out the candles. If Kim blows out all the candles, her wish will come true.

One, two, three, blow!

Happy birthday, Kim!

What Kind of Party Is That?

"Can we have a party?" asked Ann.

"Yes, we can have a party. A party is fun!" said Mom. "Who can come?"

"A lion can come," said Ann.

over

"A lion?" asked Mom.

"A princess can come," said Ann.

"A princess?" asked Mom.

"Two pirates can come. A cowboy can come. A penguin can come," said Ann.

"Two pirates? A cowboy? A penguin? What kind of party is that?" asked Mom.

"A costume party!" said Ann.

Ocean Animals

Many animals live in the _____ 5
ocean. Many animals live _____ 9
beside the ocean. _____ 12

Some ocean animals live deep _____ 17
in the water. The water is so _____ 24
deep that there is no light. _____ 30
These animals do not come _____ 35
up to the top of the ocean. _____ 42

over

Some animals live at the top _____ 48
of the ocean. Sometimes these _____ 53
animals jump out of the water. _____ 59

fin

tail

Some animals that live in _____ 64
the ocean have fins to help _____ 70
them swim. Their tails help _____ 75
them swim, too. _____ 78

shell

Some animals live in the sand _____ 84
by the ocean. Some of these _____ 90
ocean animals live in shells. _____ 95

Self-Check

1. Many animals live in the _____ .

2. Why do some ocean animals have no light?

3. Why are fins and tails important?

3. Fins and tails help ocean animals swim.

2. They live deep in the water.

1. Many animals live in the ocean.

The Ants and Their Plants

Ned and Ted Ant came in and _____ 7
said, "We got more plants. We _____ 13
have lots to eat this winter." _____ 19

Ron and Jon Ant came in _____ 25
and said, "We played bug _____ 30
tug. We had fun." _____ 34

"All you do is play, play, play," _____ 41
said Ned and Ted. "What will _____ 47
you eat this winter?" _____ 51

Winter came. Ron and Jon did _____ 57
not have many plants to eat. _____ 63

over ➤

Ron and Jon went to Ned _____69
and Ted and said, "We are _____75
sad. We ran out of plants." _____81

"You may eat some of our _____87
plants," said Ned. "But you _____92
must help next time." _____96

"Then we all will play bug _____102
tug," said Ted. _____105

Self-Check

1. **Ned and Ted got more _____.**
2. **Why did Ron and Jon run out of plants?**
3. **Do you think Ron and Jon will help next time? Why?**

3. Yes. They were sad when they ran out of plants.

2. All they did was play.

1. Ned and Ted got more plants.

All Kinds of Friends

Friends are people that you ———5
like. You do fun things with ———11
your friends. Friends make ———15
you happy. ———17

You may have one or ———22
two friends. ———24

You may have many friends. ———29

over

You make friends at school. _____ 34
These friends may be in class _____ 40
with you. _____ 42

You make friends near home. _____ 47
These friends live near you _____ 52
and play with you. _____ 56

Some friends may be in a _____ 62
club with you. Some friends _____ 67
may be on a team with you. _____ 74

You may keep some friends _____ 79
for a very long time. _____ 84

Self-Check

1. Friends are people that make you _____.

2. Where do you make friends?

3. How can you keep friends for a long time?

3. Answers will vary.

2. You make friends at school, in class, at home, in a club, and on a team.

1. Friends are people that make you happy.

F–G Audio CD Track 12

The Game

Ben and Tim are friends. Ben _____ 6
and Tim like to play games. _____ 12
They like to play What Is in _____ 19
the Box? _____ 21

"Close your eyes. Touch what _____ 26
is in the box. Guess what is _____ 33
in the box," Ben said to Tim. _____ 40

Tim closed his eyes. Tim put _____ 46
his hands into the box. Tim _____ 52
touched something round. He _____ 56
touched something fuzzy. _____ 59

over

"Is it a tennis ball?" asked Tim. _____ 66

Ben smiled. "It is *not* a tennis _____ 73
ball," Ben said to his friend. _____ 79

Then Tim felt the fuzzy ball _____ 85
move! Tim opened his eyes. _____ 90
Tim looked into the box. He _____ 96
saw a baby duck. _____ 100

"Say hello to my new pet," _____ 106
said Ben. _____ 108

Self-Check

1. What game do Ben and Tim play?

2. Why does Ben ask Tim to close his eyes?

3. Why do you think Tim opened his eyes?

1. Ben and Tim play What Is in the Box?
2. Ben wants Tim to use his sense of touch.
3. Tim felt the fuzzy ball move. He looked into the box to see why it moved.

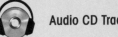

Families

There are many kinds of ____5
families. Some families are ____9
big. Some families are small. ____14

Some families live together. ____18
Some families do not. Some ____23
children live with their moms. ____28
Some live with their dads. ____33
Some children live with their ____38
grandparents. Some children ____41
live with someone else. Some ____46
families do not have children. ____51

over ➤

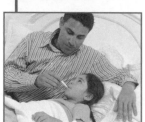

Families give us food to eat. Families give us clothes to wear. Families give us love. They take care of us when we are sick. They take us to the park to play.

57
62
67
73
80
84

The people who love you and take care of you are your family.

89
95
97

Self-Check

1. There are many kinds of _____.
2. How are food and clothes alike?
3. Why are families important?

1. There are many kinds of families.
2. Families give us food. Families give us clothes, too.
3. Families love us and take care of us.

What Goes Together?

"I drew a picture," said Dee. _____ 6
"I drew things that go together." _____ 12

"Shoes and socks go together. _____ 17
Did you draw shoes and _____ 22
socks?" asked Mom. _____ 25

"A fork and spoon go together. _____ 31
Did you draw a fork and _____ 37
spoon?" asked Dad. _____ 40

"Did you draw a ball and _____ 46
mitt?" asked Sam. _____ 49

over →

"I know! You drew a hat and gloves," said Gran.

_____ 55

_____ 59

"No, no, no, and no!" said Dee.

_____ 64

_____ 66

"What did you draw?" asked Dee's family.

_____ 71

_____ 73

"I drew us," said Dee. "We all go together."

_____ 79

_____ 82

Self-Check

1. Dee drew things that go _____.

2. Why did Dad think Dee drew a fork and spoon?

3. How do you think Dee feels about her family? Why?

1. Dee drew things that go together.
2. A fork and spoon go together.
3. Dee loves her family. She likes to draw pictures of her family.

Man at the Top of the World

The North Pole is at the top of the   9
world. The North Pole is made of snow   17
and ice. Matthew Henson was the first   24
man to stand at the top of the world.   33

Many men went on the trip with Henson.   41
Robert Peary was the leader of the trip.   49
Peary's trip started in July 1908. The trip   57
started on a ship. Then the men went by   66
sled. Dogs pulled the sleds over the snow   74
and ice.   76

over

The trip was long and hard. Henson hunted food. Henson trapped food. He fished. He used a compass to make sure everyone went the right way.

83
88
96
102

April 6, 1909, was a big day. On that day, Matthew Henson put a United States flag at the North Pole!

111
117
123

Self-Check

1. **Where is the North Pole?**

2. **How did the men travel?**

3. **Why was Matthew Henson important to the men on the trip?**

1. The North Pole is at the top of the world.

2. First, the men went by ship. Then they went by sled.

3. He hunted, trapped, and fished. He made sure everyone went the right way.

Fiction

The Ugly Duck

Little Duck wanted friends. Little Duck ___ 6
swam down the river. The ducks said, ___ 13
"Go away. You do not look like us." ___ 21

Little Duck flew north to the forest. ___ 28
The animals said, "Go away. You are ___ 35
a funny-looking duck." ___ 38

Little Duck was sad. Little Duck flew ___ 45
south to the lake. He saw some swans. ___ 53
"Swans are so pretty," said Little Duck. ___ 60

over ➡

Then Little Duck went to sleep. Little _____ 67
Duck slept for a long, long time. _____ 74

Little Duck woke up and looked at _____ 81
himself in the lake. "I do not believe _____ 89
what I am seeing," he said. _____ 95

The swans saw Little Duck, too. The _____ 102
swans said, "You are not a duck. _____ 109
You are a pretty swan. Will you be _____ 117
our friend?" _____ 119

Self-Check

1. Little Duck swam down the _____.

2. Why was Little Duck sad?

3. Why was Little Duck surprised when he looked at himself in the lake?

1. Little Duck swam down the river.

2. Little Duck was sad because the ducks told him to go away. The animals said he looked funny.

3. Little Duck saw that he was a swan, not a duck.

The First Plane Ride

People have always wanted to fly like _____ 7
birds. Orville and Wilbur Wright were _____ 13
the first people to find a way to fly _____ 22
that really worked. _____ 25

The Wright brothers loved to fly kites. _____ 32
The brothers also liked to make things. _____ 39
First, they made a glider. A glider is a _____ 48
plane without a motor. The glider was _____ 55
hard to steer in the wind. Wilbur made _____ 63
special wings for the glider. The glider _____ 70
flew in the air for 600 feet! _____ 77

over ➤

Now the brothers were ready to try
longer flights. Orville and Wilbur Wright
wanted to be the first people to fly
an airplane with a motor.

In the winter of 1903, the Wright
brothers flew the first airplane!

Self-Check

1. The Wright brothers loved to fly _____.

2. Why did Wilbur make special wings for the glider?

3. Do you think the Wright brothers are famous? Why?

1. The Wright brothers loved to fly kites.
2. The glider was hard to steer in the wind.
3. Yes. They were the first people to find a way to fly that really worked. They flew the first airplane.

The Boy Who Wanted to Fly

Long ago, a boy wanted to fly. The | 8
boy looked at the birds. The birds had | 16
wings. The boy said, "I could fly if I | 25
had wings." | 27

The boy made wings out of wax and | 35
feathers. The boy put on the wings. He | 43
climbed to the top of a tall tree. The | 52
boy jumped. He flapped his wings. He | 59
flew up, up, up. He flew up to the sun. | 69

over

When the boy got near the sun, he began to fall. The hot sun melted his wings! The boy went down, down, down.

Some big birds saw the boy falling. The birds saved the boy! The birds flew the boy up, up, up.

"Now I feel like a bird," said the boy.

Self-Check

1. A boy made wings out of _____.

2. Why did the boy fall?

3. How do you think the boy felt when the birds helped him fly? Why?

1. A boy made wings out of wax and feathers.
2. The hot sun melted his wings.
3. The boy was happy. The boy wanted to fly. He said, "Now I feel like a bird."

Nonfiction

Step 1:

Step 2:

Step 3:

Step 4:

Step 5:

Step 6:

Homemade Pizza

People in Italy made the first pizzas. ___7
Today, pizza is a favorite food around ___14
the world. You can make pizza at ___21
home. Here is how: ___25

Step 1: Buy pizza dough, tomato sauce, ___32
and shredded cheese. ___35

Step 2: Get out the tools you'll need: ___43
a spoon, pizza pan, and baking pan. ___50

over

Step 3: Open the pizza dough. Spread the dough around in the pan.   57   63

Step 4: Put some sauce on the dough. Spread the sauce around with a spoon.   71   78

Step 5: Put the cheese on top of the sauce.   86   88

Step 6: Bake the pizza at 450 degrees for 15 minutes.   96   99

Step 7: Don't forget the most important part—eat the pizza!   106   110

Self-Check

1. **Who made the first pizzas?**

2. **First you put sauce on the pizza dough. Then you put _____ on top of the sauce.**

3. **Why is it good to know how to make pizza at home?**

3. Pizza is a favorite food around the world.

2. You put cheese on top of the sauce.

1. People in Italy made the first pizzas.

Fiction

Why the Sun and the Moon Live in the Sky

A Folktale from West Africa

Long ago, Sun, Moon, and Sea were ⎯⎯ 7
friends. Sun and Moon lived in a house ⎯⎯ 15
on Earth. ⎯⎯ 17

"Come live with us, Sea. Our house will ⎯⎯ 25
be your house," said Sun and Moon. ⎯⎯ 32

"Thank you," said Sea. Sea liked living ⎯⎯ 39
with Sun and Moon. But Sea wanted ⎯⎯ 46
her friends to live in the house, too. Fish ⎯⎯ 55
came to live in the house. Birds came ⎯⎯ 63
to live in the house. ⎯⎯ 68

over

The house became crowded. Sun and
Moon left the house. They flew to the
sky to live. Soon, Sun and Moon missed
their friend Sea.

_____74
_____82
_____90
_____93

"I will watch over you all day, Sea,"
said Sun.

_____101
_____103

"I will watch over you at night, Sea,"
said Moon.

_____111
_____113

"Thank you!" said Sea. "Now I know we
will always be friends."

_____121
_____125

Self-Check

1. Sun and Moon lived in a house on _____.

2. Why did Sun and Moon fly to the sky to live?

3. What is the folktale mostly about?

1. Sun and Moon lived in a house on Earth.
2. The house became crowded.
3. The folktale is mostly about friends.

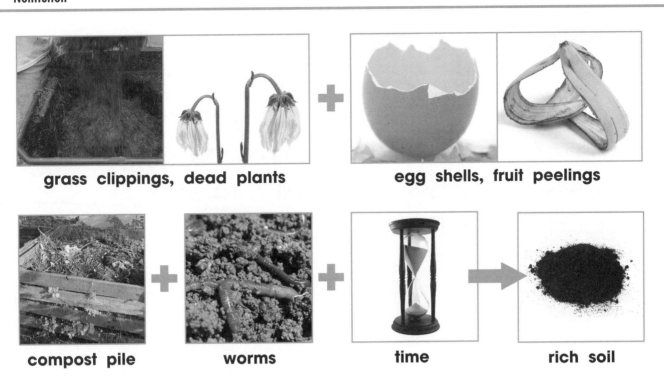

grass clippings, dead plants   egg shells, fruit peelings

compost pile   worms   time   rich soil

Make a Compost Pile

Do you know how to turn garbage into _____ 8
riches? Make a compost pile! Get grass _____ 15
clippings. Get dead leaves and plants. _____ 21
Put them in a pile outside. Over time, _____ 29
the grass, leaves, and plants will turn _____ 36
into rich dirt. _____ 39

Do you want to get richer quicker? Put _____ 47
worms in the compost pile! Worms eat _____ 54
old grass, leaves, and plants. The worms _____ 61
leave behind good soil. New plants like _____ 68
to grow in this good soil. _____ 74

over

You can put other things in the
compost pile, too. You can put in
things from the kitchen. Many people
use eggshells, fruit peelings, and
coffee grounds. These will turn into
good, rich dirt.

_____ 81
_____ 88
_____ 94
_____ 99
_____ 105
_____ 108

Self-Check

1. **You can turn garbage into _____.**

2. **Why do people put worms in a compost pile?**

3. **What could you do after you eat a banana? Why?**

1. You can turn garbage into riches.

2. Worms eat old grass, leaves, and plants. Worms leave behind good soil.

3. You could put the banana peel in a compost pile. Over time, the peel will turn into rich dirt.

Fiction

The Worm Contest

"Let's have a contest," said Bo Worm.   7
"Let's see who can eat the most."   14

Big worms and little worms entered the   21
contest. Each worm had a pile of old   29
leaves and plants to eat.   34

"Time to begin," said Grandpa Worm.   40
"One, two, three, go!"   44

The worms began to eat the leaves   51
and plants. The worms ate and ate.   58
Then the worms slowed down. Soon,   64
they could not eat another bite.   70

over

Only Bo Worm kept eating. Bo was _____ 77
hungry. He ate and ate until his pile _____ 85
was gone. _____ 87

"Bo wins the prize!" said Grandpa Worm. _____ 94

"What's the prize?" asked Bo. _____ 99

"A pile of old leaves and plants," said _____ 107
Grandpa Worm. _____ 109

"Hooray!" said Bo. "I'm still hungry!" _____ 115

Self-Check

1. Who entered the contest?

2. Why did Bo Worm keep eating?

3. What do you think Bo will do next? Why?

1. Big worms and little worms entered the contest.

2. Bo was hungry.

3. Bo will eat his prize. He is still hungry.

Happy Thanksgiving

Long ago, Pilgrims came to America.　　6
The Pilgrims did not have much to eat.　　14
They did not know how to grow food　　22
in their new home.　　26

Native peoples made friends with the　　32
Pilgrims. The native peoples helped the　　38
Pilgrims. They showed the Pilgrims how　　44
to grow food.　　47

over ➤

The Pilgrims and native peoples got together for a big meal. The Pilgrims gave thanks for the food. They gave thanks for their new friends.

53
60
67
72

We still remember the Pilgrims. We remember the native peoples who helped them, too. We have a holiday called Thanksgiving. Families get together for a big meal. Families eat foods that the Pilgrims and native peoples ate. Families give thanks for food and friends.

78
83
90
95
103
109
116

Self-Check

1. The Pilgrims did not have much to _____.

2. What happened after the native peoples helped the Pilgrims?

3. Why is Thanksgiving a special holiday in the United States?

3. People remember the Pilgrims and native peoples.

2. The Pilgrims and native peoples got together for a big meal.

1. The Pilgrims did not have much to eat.

Fiction

Ma's Runaway Pumpkin

Ma wanted to make a pumpkin pie for _____ 8
Thanksgiving. Ma went to the garden. _____ 14
The pumpkin Ma picked began to roll _____ 21
away. "Stop!" Ma cried. _____ 25

The pumpkin rolled out of the garden. _____ 32
Ma ran after the pumpkin. The pumpkin _____ 39
rolled across the field and down the _____ 46
hill. Ma could not catch the pumpkin. _____ 53

The pumpkin rolled faster and faster. _____ 59
Finally, it rolled into a tree. Bam! The _____ 67
pumpkin broke into pieces. _____ 71

over ➤

Some mice saw the broken pumpkin. _____ 77
"Dinner!" said the mice. _____ 81

Ma looked and looked for the runaway _____ 88
pumpkin. Finally, she saw the pumpkin. _____ 94
"There you are!" she said. _____ 99

The mice looked at Ma. Ma ran at the _____ 108
mice. They were too full to run away. _____ 116
Then Ma smiled. "Happy Thanksgiving!" _____ 121
Ma said. _____ 123

Self-Check

1. **Why did Ma want a pumpkin?**

2. **What did Ma do when the pumpkin began to roll away?**

3. **How do you know Ma was not mad?**

1. To make a pumpkin pie for Thanksgiving.
2. Ma ran after the pumpkin.
3. Ma smiled and said "Happy Thanksgiving!" to the mice.

Fossils

Fossils are what is left of animals and plants ___9
that lived long, long ago. Fossils tell us things ___18
about the past. Fossils can even tell us what ___27
dinosaurs looked like. ___30

There are many different kinds of fossils. There ___38
are fossils of teeth and bones. There are fossils of ___48
footprints. There are fossils of shells and plants. ___56

over ➤

Fossils form in different ways. Some fossils form _____64
in water. First, an animal dies in the water. _____73
Soon, only the bones and teeth are left. Over _____82
time, sand and clay cover the bones and teeth. _____91
Later, the water dries up. Then the bones turn _____100
into rock. _____102

Some fossils are buried in the ground. Do you _____111
want to find a fossil? Get digging! _____118

Self-Check

1. There are many different _____ of fossils.

2. What happens after bones and teeth are left in water?

3. Why are fossils important?

1. There are many different kinds of fossils.
2. Sand and clay cover the bones and teeth.
3. Fossils tell us things about the past.

Fiction

The Big Tree

Tom and Dad were walking in the woods. "Look! _____9
Look at this tree on the ground," said Dad. _____18

"This is a big tree," said Tom. "It must be _____28
very old." _____30

Dad said, "We can tell how old the tree is. Look _____41
at the lines on the tree trunk. The lines make rings _____52
inside the trunk. Look at the spaces between the _____61
rings. That is how much the tree grew each year." _____71

"Let's count the rings on the trunk," said Tom. _____80

over ➤

Dad and Tom counted the rings. "The tree is fifty years old," said Tom. 89 94

"I'm fifty years old, also," said Dad. 101

"I'm glad you didn't grow as much as the tree!" said Tom. 111 113

Self-Check

1. Tom and Dad were walking in the ____.

2. Why did Tom think the tree was very old?

3. What can you tell from the rings on a tree trunk?

3. Each ring stands for one year of the tree's age.

2. The tree was big.

1. Tom and Dad were walking in the woods.

The Price of Peaches

Peaches grow on trees. Peach trees need water _____8
to grow. Sometimes rain gives peach trees all the _____17
water they need. _____20

Sometimes the peach trees do not get much _____28
rain. Then farmers must water the trees. Some _____36
farmers bring water to the trees in pipes. This _____45
is called irrigation. _____48

When the peaches are fully grown, farmers send _____56
them to stores. The more peaches the stores have _____65
for sale, the less the peaches cost. _____72

over ➤

Sometimes the peach trees get too much rain. _____80
Too much water is bad for peaches. Some of the _____90
peaches rot, so farmers do not have as many to _____100
send to the stores. The fewer peaches the stores _____109
have for sale, the more the peaches cost. _____117

Self-Check

1. **Where do peaches grow?**

2. **Why do some farmers use irrigation?**

3. **You go to the store. The price of peaches is low. What can you tell?**

1. Peaches grow on trees.
2. Sometimes the peach trees do not get much rain.
3. The peaches got the right amount of water. Farmers had many peaches to send to the stores.

Fiction

The King Who Loved Gold

Long ago, a king had some gold. "I love gold," _____10
said the king. "I wish that everything I touch _____19
would turn to gold." _____23

The king got his wish. He touched a flower. The _____33
flower turned to gold! He touched a tree. The tree _____43
turned to gold! He touched his food. The food _____52
turned to gold! _____55

"This is wonderful!" said the king. "Now I REALLY _____64
love gold!" _____66

The king's daughter came into the room. She _____74
had her teddy bear. "Good night, Daddy," said _____82
the little girl. _____85

over →

The king hugged his little girl. She turned to gold! ⎯⎯⎯ 95

"Oh no!" said the king. "I do not love gold as ⎯⎯⎯ 106
much as I love my little girl! I wish more than ⎯⎯⎯ 117
anything to have my little girl back!" ⎯⎯⎯ 124

The king got his wish, and he never wished for ⎯⎯⎯ 134
more gold again. ⎯⎯⎯ 137

Self-Check

1. A king had some ____.

2. Why did the little girl turn to gold?

3. How did the king's feelings change?

3. At first, the king wanted everything to be gold. Then he realized he loved his little girl more than gold. The king hugged his little girl.

2. Everything the king touched turned to gold.

1. A king had some gold.

Fluency Self-Assessment Master Checklist

☺ ☹

Speed/Pacing

Did my speed and pacing match the kind of text I was reading? ☐ ☐

Did my speed and pacing match what the author was saying? ☐ ☐

Did I read with a natural talking voice? ☐ ☐

Did I slow my reading down when appropriate? ☐ ☐

Did I pay attention to punctuation? ☐ ☐

Pausing

Did I pause to keep from running all my words together? ☐ ☐

Did I pause in the correct locations? ☐ ☐

Did I pause for the appropriate length of time? ☐ ☐

Did I pause to help my reading make sense? ☐ ☐

Did I use punctuation to help me figure out when to pause? ☐ ☐

Inflection/Intonation

Did I make my voice rise at a question mark? ☐ ☐

Did I make my voice fall at a period? ☐ ☐

Did I think about what the author was saying so I would
know when to read louder or softer? ☐ ☐

Did I think about what the author was saying so I would know
when to stress or emphasize words? ☐ ☐

Phrasing

Did I notice the phrases? ☐ ☐

Did I read all the words in each phrase together? ☐ ☐

Did I think about what the words in the phrase mean when
they are together? ☐ ☐

Expression

Did I look for clues so I could anticipate the mood of the passage? ☐ ☐

Did I use my tone of voice, facial expressions, and body language
to express what the author or characters were thinking or feeling? ☐ ☐

Did I change my reading when something new was about to happen? ☐ ☐

Integration

Did I read the words right? (accuracy) ☐ ☐

Did I read the words at the right speed? (rate) ☐ ☐

Did I read with expression? (prosody) ☐ ☐

Did my reading sound like talking? ☐ ☐

Did I understand what I read? ☐ ☐

My Fluency Practice Graph • Grade 1

Name: _____   Level: _____

Card: _____   Reading Rate Goal: _____

Color in the graph to show how many words you read in one minute.

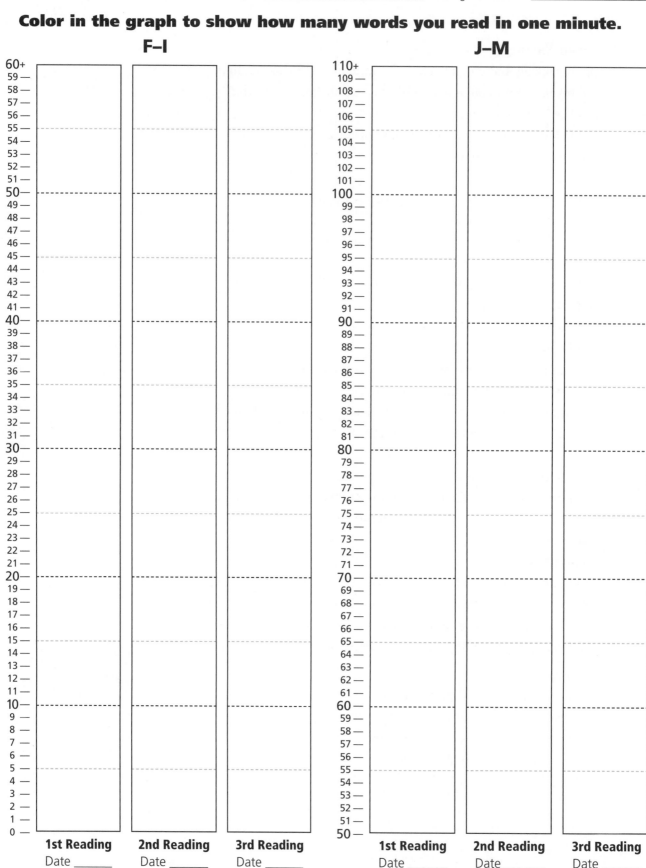

My Fluency Practice Graph • Grade 1

Name: _____   Level: _____

Card: _____   Reading Rate Goal: _____

Color in the graph to show how many words you read in one minute.

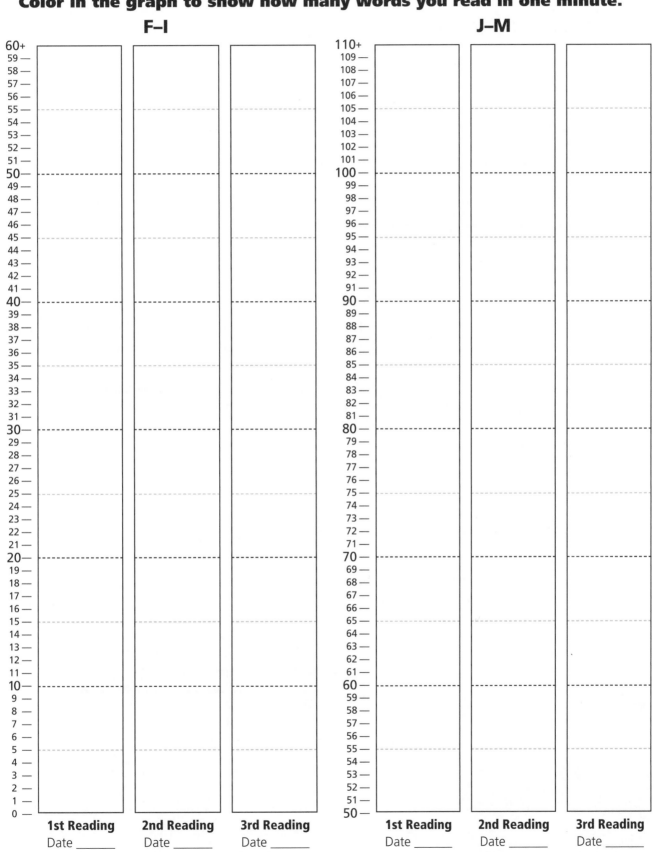

F–I

J–M

Student Instructions

1. Choose a fiction or nonfiction passage for your level.

2. Put the audio CD into the CD player. Look at the top right corner of the passage. Find the track numbers for the passage.

3. Listen to the fluent track on the audio CD. Follow along.

4. Play the fluent track again. Read along quietly with the audio CD. Repeat if you need more practice.

5. Read the passage aloud quietly several times without the audio CD.

6. For Levels F–M, answer the Self-Check questions at the end of the passage. Check your answers by reading the answers printed upside-down on the page. Make sure you understand what you read.

7. Ask a grown-up or buddy to time your reading with the stopwatch. Read for one minute. Mark the correct word rate to the right of your passage.

8. Mark your score on the My Fluency Practice Graph. Color in the graph.

9. Look at the chart below. Did you read with fluency? If the answer is NO, practice and read the same passage again. If the answer is YES, pick a new passage for your level. Use the Fluency Self-Assessment Master Checklist to help you choose skills you would like to improve.

Practice Makes Perfect!

Reading Rate Goals			
Grade	Words Per Minute		
	Fall	Winter	Spring
1		23	53
2	51	72	89
3	71	92	107